BEYOND THE JOB DESCRIPTION

How to Succeed in the Workplace

Christina N. Alva | Camille Marbury

Published by Amazing Books, LLC.
Contact: ChristinaAlva.com
info@ChristinaAlva.com

The information contained within this book is strictly for educational purposes. If you wish to apply ideas contained herein, you are taking full responsibility for your actions. The guidance provided within this book was developed based on the personal experiences and opinions of the authors. The authors do not assume and hereby disclaim any liability to any party for any loss, damage, or disruption caused by errors or omissions, whether such errors or omissions result from accident, negligence, or any other cause.

Publishing Coordination by Brown & Duncan Brand. BandDBrand.com

Illustrations by Rebecca Oh
www.rebeccaoh.com @rebeccaohart

ISBN: 978-0-9992023-1-9

Printed in the United States of America

Acknowledgements

Christina

I would like to acknowledge Tressa Azarel, @ceoazarel, for her encouragement and motivation. Her advice and can-do attitude helped me to realize my dream of becoming an author while fulfilling my passion of helping others succeed.

Camille

I would like to thank and acknowledge my dear friend and mentor, Thelma Williams, for her relentless encouragement, genuine concern and care for my well-being, and continual motivation to be my best self. She truly helped me to realize my endless possibilities and to DO GREAT things! I plan to do just that while helping others do the same. I also want to thank and publicly acknowledge my best friend and sister, Christina Alva, who helps keep me in check with her T.I.L.T. (inside joke) advice and full embodiment of Philippians 4:13; my wonderful and super chill nephew, Andrew Alva, Jr.; my brilliant sister and ace, Candace Marbury; and my witty and cool brother-in-law, Christopher Farmer. Thank you, Candace and Chris, for your tremendous feedback during this endeavor. Go FarBury!

Big thanks to my God, who is the head of my life; my parents; and my continuous flow of family and friends who get me.

May the journey be long, the moments captured, and the achievement strides continue!

Dedication

We dedicate this book to everyone who has sat at work and thought to themselves, 'I don't get paid enough for this', and to all those who are entering the workplace for the first time or returning to work and looking for guidance on making the most of it.

Testimonials

"Christina's tips for writing effective resumes and interviewing like a boss helped me land my dream job. When I was struggling at work, she knew exactly what I was going through. Her advice has helped me get through some tough times and even get a promotion." – **Maria H.**

"I was fortunate to have Christina as a supervisor for my first job after graduate school. I remember her being actively engaged in mentoring me about numerous topics that include work professionalism, networking, data analytics, and even life skills. One of the many words of advice that stands out to me is to always find a mentor in my current work environment. This has benefited me to this day." – **Alexis A.**

"Camille has always been my go-to-person. She is very knowledgeable and resourceful; and if she doesn't have the answer, she will get the answer for you. Camille has also encouraged me to develop myself personally and professionally, and is a great support. I'm honored to have her as my friend." – **Michelle R.**

TABLE *of* CONTENTS

Introduction

It was my first day on the job, and I arrived twenty minutes early. The night before, I laid out my brand-new suit, set my alarm, and completed my welcome paperwork. I went to bed early so that I could get a good night's rest, but the excitement kept me up most of the night. All kinds of questions were running through my mind. How should I wear my hair? What if I arrive too early? Is there such a thing as too early? Should I take a lunch? Should I buy lunch? How should I greet my boss? What if they ask me to do something I don't know how to do? What if they feel they hired the wrong person? After going through the motions, I assured myself, 'I am ready. This is what I have prepared for. All of the studying and all the good grades prepared me for this—my dream job.' Finally, I fell asleep.

A few days passed, and I started to settle in. I met several people in the office who seemed friendly. My computer was all set up and I was ready to prove myself. When I received my first task, I was eager to impress the higher ups. So, after jotting down a few notes on my notepad, I smiled and told my supervisor, "Got it. I will get this done right away." I went back to my desk and stared at my notes for a moment and then took a deep breath. I had no idea what to do. I didn't even know how to begin. What now? School did not prepare me for this.

When I started applying for jobs, I quickly reached out to my sister, Camille, and begged her to help me. She, being the oldest, had already obtained a job as an auditor right after college. Now that I was entering the workforce, I knew that she had all the answers to help me land a job. Camille was always very professional in her demeanor and she looked and acted like a successful business woman. I, on the other hand, was more free-spirited and undisciplined. I needed her to teach me how to write a resume and sound smart when I spoke, so that I would not come across an idiot in an interview. Camille, being the awesome big sister that she is, assisted me in every part of the job search process and helped me land a position with the federal government. Since then, I have watched her help many young people through mentoring, volunteering to lead youth groups, and by helping them to perfect their resumes and land dream jobs. I too started mentoring and coaching others in the areas in which my sister helped me. We have both held jobs in the state and federal governments, and the private sector (i.e. "Corporate America"). As a supervisor and recruiter, I regularly deal with professionals entering the workplace for the first time. I have seen the nervous ticks, the blank stares when they are asked to complete tasks they really don't understand how to do, and have worked closely with individuals to help them gain confidence and grow in the workplace.

~

My sister, Christina, gives me too much credit, but I am the first born! The fact that I am the older sister means that I have had to grin and bear it, so to speak, when it comes to getting things done. Without an older sibling, I had to glean and research a lot of information for myself. Parents don't always remember what things were like when they were starting out, and in a constantly changing world, their advice may no longer be relevant. Having to set the example isn't always easy, but I had a natural desire to pass on the knowledge that I learned every step of the way. I love helping others, especially if it means I can spare them from making mistakes, falling on their faces, getting fired, or being humiliated. I do have to admit that I have turned to my sisters, Christina and Candace (the youngest), now that they are further along in their careers for tips on a regular basis. Like the Proverb says, "Iron sharpens iron," and I am always looking to improve and I love being around others that like to do the same.

Our desire is to help professionals feel confident and perform effectively in the workplace. We wrote this book to share advice on the workplace duties that schools do not teach. How do you succeed in the workplace? What do you need to do to ensure that you become or continue to be a top performer and get promoted?

What tips and guidelines should you follow? This book will outline top tips for you to practice in order to improve your performance in the workplace. It will provide you with strategies for interviewing, analyzing your strengths and weaknesses as it relates to your work performance, the importance of communication, how to conduct yourself in the workplace, and how to read your paycheck.

We want to help you avoid common mistakes made by so many and provide you with tools to help you be successful. We hope you enjoy this book and we wish you great success in your career!

Chapter 1

Interviewing Like a BOSS

Chances are you've been on several interviews, or you have sent your resume out to dozens of potential employers and you are waiting to land an interview for your dream job, or perhaps you've found a "job," but it's not the ideal position for the career goals that you have. No matter which side of the coin you fall on, this section will help you interview like a boss. This section will cover everything you need to know from tips to improve your resume and when to apply to equipping you with skills to ACE your next interview.

The Resume

Before we talk about interviewing, we have to say a few things about resumes. Your resume is the first impression recruiters will have of you. We recommend tailoring your resume to the position you are applying for before submitting it. When using an objective statement, make sure that it fits the positing to which you are applying. For example, if you are applying for a position as a statistician, you do not want your objective to read, "Newly graduated economics major seeking full-time employment as a financial consultant" or, "Motivated individual seeking full-time employment as a Teacher within your University." You get the point, right?

Make sure you have the proper resume format for the position. A resume for a federal government position is usually different from the format you would use for applying for a non-government position. Likewise, a resume for a job in finance may be different from that of a job as a sales manager (which may include stats and other types of references). If you are posting your resume on common job search websites like Career Builder or Monster, you will want to refresh your resume often. Some recruiters frequently check these sites and pull the most recently submitted resumes. When you refresh your resume, it is moved to the top of the pile. Therefore, doing this regularly will ensure that your resume gets the most views. Be mindful of headhunters! Headhunters are companies that search for people on behalf of other organizations. If you have ever posted your resume on LinkedIn, then you may know what we are talking about. When your resume contains certain key words that meet an employer's needs, a headhunter or recruiter may reach out to you via email to see if you are interested in a position they think will suit you well. They find keywords in your resume and profile and match those to the descriptions of the job postings for which they are recruiting.

Check your online profiles to ensure that you have a detailed resume with 'key words' to help headhunters and recruiters match you to ideal positions. For example, as a programmer, you would include key words of the different programming languages that you know, in addition to your years of experience with each language, the different platforms you know, and the types of data you have mastered. These details will ensure that you are not contacted for a dental position.

Social media, in general, is very important when applying for jobs. Many companies have recruiters that search through LinkedIn and other social media sites to find candidates that may be suited for positions that are difficult to fill. Aside from your resume, social media provides an impression to recruiters, so use it wisely. If a recruiter were hiring a candidate for a customer service position and viewed that person's Facebook or Instagram page and saw that the potential candidate was involved in several team sport activities and social clubs and had many positive posts, the recruiter could get the sense that the applicant works well with people. The job applicant would also appear to be likeable. This is an example of where social media can help in the recruiting process. On the other hand, if a recruiter or administrator wanted to hire a high school teacher and saw Facebook pictures of the applicant drunk and passed out in public, obscene gestures, and foul language, the recruiter may conclude that this individual is not someone who should teach impressionable teenagers. What you post on social media will establish your personal brand either positively or negatively. When hiring someone to represent a company, the hiring manager wants to make sure the applicant will be a positive representative. New employees are investments to the company; in this business game, nobody wants to make a negative bet.

On several occasions, I (Christina) have had to look through stacks of resumes. It is not easy going through about one hundred resumes to find the one person who would best fit the one position for which I am hiring. Here is some insight into the process. For an entry-level position, let's say there are fifty-seven recent graduates in the pile all applying for the same position. How do you cut that pile down? Some may be thinking grade point average (GPA). Others may be thinking experience. Both of these are good options. As the hiring manager, I know what the position would require. Although a high GPA is a good indicator of performance, experience is the greatest teacher and very valuable in the recruiting process. Experience shows that you have had an opportunity to perform for someone else who can vouch for you.

It shows that you have taken what you have learned in the classroom and applied it to real world situations. When looking at the stack of resumes in our example skill set, experience and GPA help cut down the fifty-seven resumes to about five. From there, phone screens and in-person interviews helped to make the final choice. This is why resumes are so important. Without a great looking resume, you may never make it to the phone screening or in-person interview. My example only contained fifty-seven applicants, but most real-world scenarios are much higher than that. Your competition increases when the company you are applying to is popular or when the position you are applying to does not require a specific skill set.

If you are in college, internships can be vital to your resume. They provide you an opportunity to experience the day-to-day environment in your industry of choice. Not only do they give you an inside look at your possible future, but they also afford you the opportunity to gain real world, on-the-job experience that employers find extremely valuable. Internships are beneficial for you, because recruiters can speak with professionals you have worked with who can attest to or validate your performance. Internships are not all about receiving a paycheck while you are in college. Even unpaid positions will provide an invaluable return on your future opportunities. You should view internship opportunities as an investment in your future. You get the chance to net work with others in your field and to find someone who wants to see you succeed and help you in your future endeavors. Interning can also help to create a relationship with a company, which can lead to future employment.

References are individuals who you have worked for or within the past who can provide additional information about your work habits, skillset, and character. They are a crucial part of your resume. Your employer may request your references with your resume or after the interview. Be sure to select individuals that you know will provide positive feedback about you to recruiters. You don't have control over what a reference will say to a recruiter, but you do have control over whom you choose. It is also a good idea to contact such individuals for permission prior to using them as a reference and to let them know they may be contacted. There is nothing more frustrating than being listed as a contact for someone, job or otherwise, and not being asked beforehand. Not doing so can result in the reference providing a negative view of you to the recruiter or not picking up the phone at all when contacted.

Cover Letters

A cover letter provides you with a way to highlight how your skills match with the job and person the company wants to hire. Cover letters are more detailed than resumes. Think of the cover letter as a bragging tool to help you distinguish yourself from other applicants. It is not meant to be a tell-all novel. The cover letter should complement your resume, not repeat it. Keep in mind that the purpose of a cover letter is to highlight your skills and experience as it relates to the needs of the hiring manager. Within the letter, indicate the position you would like and be sure to reference the company.

A typical cover letter includes the following:

1. Header – As with most letters, the cover letter starts with a header which identifies your contact information (mailing address, phone number, and email address); the recipient's contact information (contact's name, if known, company name, and mailing address); and the date.

2. Greeting – If you know the hiring manager's name, you can begin with 'Dear Dr., Mr., or Ms., followed by their last name. If the contact's name is unknown, address your letter with 'Dear Hiring Manager.'

3. Content – After your greeting, provide the content of your cover letter. The content of the letter is composed of three main parts: introductory, main, and closing paragraphs. Below are some additional tips for each content component.

~ *Introductory Paragraph* – The introductory paragraph should get the reader's attention; in two to three sentences, state the job for which you are applying and how your specific skills and experience match the needs of the company and/or position.

~ *Main Paragraph(s)* – In one or two additional paragraphs, you should explain why you are interested in the job and why you are a good fit for the position. Don't just reiterate your skills and experience that relate to the position, but state how and why and provide examples. Make sure that the skills and experience you are detailing are the ones that you briefly mentioned in your introductory paragraph so that everything flows.

~ *Closing Paragraph* – In the closing paragraph, reiterate how you would be a good fit for the company and/or position. You should also indicate that you would like the opportunity to interview and discuss employment opportunities.

4. Signature – Your letter should include a polite closing with 'Respectfully,' 'Sincerely,' or 'Thank you,' followed by your typed name and contact information (that is, your phone number and email address). If you provide your letter manually, leave space to sign your name above where your typed name and contact information are located.

Keep in mind that, like your resume, your cover letter should be tailored to each position for which you are applying. Company and hiring manager needs differ from job to job and you don't want to be overlooked simply because you did not tailor your cover letter for the position.

When to Apply

The ideal time to apply for a job depends on your preferred industry. For government and federal jobs, you should apply a year in advance. These jobs can take longer to secure. The process for any position that requires any kind of security clearance is longer than usual, so we recommend applying at least six months in advance of your desired start date. If you are in college, then you should start applying for jobs one year before graduating. You should also inquire about a company's interview process when you apply. Some companies have a multi-part interview process, which can take a few weeks to a few months. Knowing and understanding the interview and selection process can help you plan and apply accordingly.

How to Apply

Technology has made it easy for us to apply for jobs without even leaving our homes. There was a time when people actually had to leave their homes and go to a business to obtain a job application. This may still be the case for some (few) employers who are not participating in the world of technology. If applying online, be sure to have a soft copy (that is, electronic) of your resume handy so that you can attach it to your online application if the option is available. You may also want to attach a cover letter to indicate your interest in obtaining a position with the company. Refer to the *'The Resume'* and *'Cover Letter'* sections previously discussed for additional tips on these elements.

Types of Interviews

There are several different types of interviews, and nowadays, you should be prepared for in-person, telephone, and even video conference interviews.

- There are technical interviews for technical positions. For example, if applying for a software developer or programming position, you may be asked to code during the interview or participate in a code review.
- In non-technical, customer service type interviews, be prepared to answer how you would respond to several situations. These are also referred to as behavioral interviews.
- In professional interviews where you interview in person, prepare to sit and talk with several key staff includ ing your future boss.

Interviews can last anywhere from thirty minutes to several days. Most interviews in corporate America take a couple of hours. They often start with a preliminary phone screening followed by a second round where the applicant is invited into the office to meet in person. Interviewing can be scary, and sitting in front of people you don't know can be intimidating. Despite the butterflies or sinking feeling you may experience, it is important to appear FEARLESS. Be confident in yourself and your abilities. Practice in front of the mirror, beforehand, so you are aware of your facial expressions and posture. Remember to look your interviewers in the eyes and speak confidently. It's also important to be familiar with the company you are interviewing with. Take time to prepare before the interview by researching the company. You would hate to walk into an interview with McDonald's and tell them you love their Whopper.

The Interview Process

There are different interview methods depending on the industry you would like to enter. An initial phone screening will be the first step in the interviewing process for most positions. These are often conducted by a recruiting team member, which could be anyone from a human resources (HR) representative, a supervisor within the company, or a representative from a staffing agency. The next step is the in-person interview. If you move on to this step, a company may invite you onsite to meet with several key people in the company. Often, this team of people will be whom you will interact with the most once hired. Interviews in this setting may be conducted as a joint interview or in an open, panel-style setting where you sit down with three to five people and they ask you questions. It could also be a series of smaller sized meetings, for example, three or four back-to-back meetings with one to two people. Technical positions may require an onsite or on-camera live technical test as well. This is usually for software developers and programmers. Most companies only require one in-person interview; however, for technical positions you may have three or four meetings/interactions with or without an in-person interview depending on the hiring manager's preference or company hiring practices.

With more and more companies allowing employees to work from home or offsite at remote locations, in-person interviews aren't always guaranteed. For in-person interviews, it is important to know that the interview starts the moment you walk into the building and lasts until you walk out. Talking disrespectfully to someone you pass by in the halls or the front desk representative could count against you.

Why In-person Interviews?

There are several reasons for in-person interviews. They

help recruiters gauge how you interact with others, how well you speak and communicate, how you handle pressure situations, your promptness and professionalism, and your outer appearance and personal image. This is extremely important if you are applying for a position where you will be representing the company in front of clients. In-person interviews help the employer confirm that you are as sharp as you were during your initial phone screening, which is what got you through to this step in the process.

How to Dress for an Interview

For all professional interviews, a dark suit will do fine. This means a black, dark blue, gray, or navy pant or skirt suit. You should also wear shoes that are dark in color, cleaned, and polished, if needed. For women, closed toe pumps or flats are appropriate with low cut manicured (meaning clean) nails, and minimal jewelry (small earrings or studs) work best. Skirts should be long enough to sit comfortably in a chair with the hem right above, at, or below the knee. Women should also wear nice and neat hairstyles. Remember, your in-person interview could take all day, so be sure to dress business professional, but comfortable. The goal is to impress. If you are doing an on-camera interview, you still want to dress business professional and consider the camera's range. There is nothing worse than being dressed well from the waist up and then standing up and letting the camera catch your pajama pants. Depending on the type of job you are applying for, it may be acceptable to consider alternative outfits when applying. For example, if you are applying for a job as a cashier at a fast food restaurant, you could wear nice slacks with a clean polo or ironed button-down dress shirt. However, if you are applying for the manager position at the fast food restaurant, you may want to up your game a little. There's a famous quote that says you should dress for the job you want.

How to Prepare for an Interview

It is helpful to get with someone and execute a mock interview. Whether this is your first interview or your one hundredth, have a friend or family member sit down with you and role play as a recruiter. Most colleges have mock interview sessions to help students prepare for interviews. Practicing will help you become aware of your strengths and weaknesses. For example, you may find that you talk with your hands, have a nervous tick, or ramble on and get off subject when you don't have a prepared or on-the-fly response to a question. All these things can be identified in a mock interview. When preparing for the interview, you should also develop a few questions for your interviewer.

Some good questions to ask your interviewer include:

1. Can you tell me a little about your career here at the company?

2. What is the retention rate?

3. What does the average day for someone in this position look like?

Another good idea is to do some research on the company before going into the interview. It is always impressive when an interviewee can initiate a discussion about current company strategies and work initiatives. It shows that the interviewee is really interested in the company.

Here is a list of questions you can practice answering:

1. Why are you interested in working here?

2. Tell me about your last position (or an internship if you didn't have a prior position)?

3. What kinds of things are you looking to do here?

4. Have you ever worked in a team environment before?

5. What salary range are you looking for?

This one is important. You should know the position you are applying for and what the average salary is. You can search the Internet for similar positions and find salary information. In most cases, you can negotiate your salary, but to do so you need to be well informed about what the position is worth. Be sure to provide a reasonable salary range. Asking for a $100,000 annual salary for a position that has an average salary of $60,000 could turn away your interviewers.

6. What would you say your strengths and weaknesses are?

7. Can you tell us a little bit about yourself?

8. What are your hobbies?

Practicing a response to these questions is a good start to preparing for your interview. There will be several other questions that are more specific to the position. Overall, you want to maintain a professional demeanor and display confidence while assuring the interviewers that you have the skills and desire to do the job better than all their other candidates.

Interview Do's and Don'ts

1. **Do** be on time. If you have a scheduled phone screening, check that your phone is working in advance, and be sure that you can take the call in a private place where there is no background noise and you can be heard clearly. Make sure you are in place and ready to receive your phone call five to ten minutes before the scheduled time. If you are traveling to an in-person interview, you want to arrive fifteen to thirty minutes early. Allow yourself extra time to travel and get settled before your scheduled interview. You don't want to arrive right on time, all out of breath, and anxious because you thought you might be late. You want to have a firm handshake, look your interviewer in the eyes when responding to questions, speak confidently, know your resume and skill set, be articulate (speak clearly), and be direct and to the point (that is, concise).

2. **Do** keep good posture, smile often, and know how you respond when you are nervous. For example, if you tend to speak quickly when you are nervous, practice speaking slower.

3. **Do** inquire about next steps. At the end of your interview, if you have not discussed this already you can

ask what will happen next in the process and for the contact information of the interviewer. When asked for contact information, some interviewers will provide you with a business card, whereas others will provide you with their phone number or email address. It is also okay to contact the HR department and ask about the status of your application to follow up.

4. **Do** take notes. Some interviews may be conducted in several one-on-one meetings. When this is the case, you may have time between interviews to write down key discussion items that can assist you in writing a thank-you note later. For panel interviews, try to write down key takeaways as soon as you can for the same purpose. These notes will come in handy and help you to stick out in the interviewers' minds because you can reconnect key discussion points, remind them of who you are, and reiterate why you are interested in working with them.

5. **Do not** stray from the topic or question presented to you. Sometimes interviewees can avoid answering a question or go off into left field on a rant about something unrelated to the question asked. Try not to talk with your hands. If this is a habit of yours, try sitting on your hands or keeping them crossed in your lap.

You can also try holding a notebook, which can be used to carry extra copies of your resume.

6. **Do not** interrupt the interviewer.

7. **Do not** give a guess response when you do not under stand or know the answer to the question being asked. Interviewers can tell when applicants don't know what they are talking about. It is better to just respond with something like, "That's a good question, I will have to get back to you on that;" "I don't know;" or "I am not familiar with that."

8. **Do not** forget your manners. If you are on a lunch interview, although this may sound funny, do not eat off anyone else's plate, do not talk about bodily functions or illnesses, and do not make comments about how you are taking a sick day from your current job in order to attend the interview. Lunch interviews are set up to be more informal, but they are still part of the interview process. Be prepared to answer questions, and remember that your goal is to make *a good* impression.

Robbie thinks he is on time for his 9 a.m. interview. He is just arriving. He should have arrived at 8:40 to give himself time to calm down, get organized, and prepare mentally for his interview. First impressions are crucial. If you were standing on the other side of that door about to meet Robbie, what would your first impression be?

Chapter 2
Workplace Habits

The way you carry yourself at work is important, especially if you are new and trying to establish yourself. One bad habit that new employees develop is being late. Showing up every day around ten in the morning when you have a nine to five work schedule is not a good look. Always remember that what you do during the workday and how you do it can open or close doors to opportunities. Remember that you are always "on." This is key. You must realize (from the time when you first join an organization) that you are *always* being watched. Managers are evaluating your activities, interactions, and the posture and attitude you maintain when you are in the workplace.

Set Your Alarm

Pay attention to what time you arrive to work and what time you leave, because you can bet that somebody else will. Do not give anyone a reason to fire you or to complain to management. Little things like this can be your downfall. You can be a great performer and only mess up by arriving late, and yet get terminated. Most jobs require you to put in a set amount of hours each day. A standard forty-hour week requires one to work, for example, eight hours per day, five days a week. That does not include your lunch break. Add lunch in and depending on a thirty-minute or one-hour lunch, you have an eight and a half or nine hour workday. This can vary if you have an alternate work schedule approved by your supervisor or if you are a part-time employee. If your hours are nine in the morning to five in the evening, taking an hour lunch period means you work until six in the evening. Let me be real clear. Being on time (for your nine o'clock in the morning shift) does not mean you are parking your car in the garage or walking through the door at 9 a.m. It means you are in your chair working at the start of your shift. It's the same for when you leave at the end of the day. Leaving at six o'clock in the evening does not mean you are in your car at that time on your way to happy hour. It means you finished your assigned tasks and are stopping at six o'clock in the evening. Sometimes we run late, and that's understandable.

The key word is *sometimes*, not every day. It shouldn't even be once a week. If you come in a few minutes late, then you need to stay a few minutes late to ensure that you work your full shift (typically eight hours). Again, as a new person in the company, someone is watching you. It is important to note that as you move up in your company the rules may not remain so strict. The point is that you are new and still trying to make a name for yourself. You need to paint the picture that you want your job and that you want to work. Arriving late and leaving early sends the message that you have other things that you would rather be doing. Well guess what, there are other people out there who would gladly take your place and show up on time.

As you consider your work hours, remember not to compare yourself to what someone else is doing. Don't use the excuse, 'Well this person comes in late all the time and leaves early, so why can't I?' Don't worry about what anyone else is doing. You don't know their situation. You are responsible for your own actions. By the way, most businesses today require you to swipe an identification badge to enter the workplace. In addition, computers that require employees to sign in are likely tracking their hours and activity on the computers. With today's technology, both devices can be used to track your start and stop time for the workday.

If you have trouble arriving to work early, which means on time, try some of these techniques:

- Tell yourself that your workday starts thirty minutes before it actually does. Trick your mind into thinking you start at 8:30 a.m. instead of 9:00 a.m. so that you get into the habit of being thirty minutes early. When you get to work early, you can take your time and prepare for the day, eat breakfast, or catch up with other coworkers (assuming that this is acceptable).

- Set multiple alarms. If you are like many people and you turn your alarm off when it beeps, try setting a couple of alarms so that you don't accidently oversleep. You can also set your alarm on two different devices with one close to your bed and the second out of arms reach so that you have to get out of the bed to turn it off.
- Carpool. It puts the pressure on you to be on time so you don't make someone else late. Of course, this means you can't carpool with someone who is habitually late.
- Go to bed. Stop staying up late playing video games, watching television, and scrolling social media websites like Instagram and YouTube. Although these things are fun, there's always another level to conquer, another show to watch, and another post to read. You can waste a lot of time.
- Change your work schedule. Find out if it is possible to change your work schedule. For example, change it from 8:00 a.m. to 5:00 p.m. to 9:00 a.m. to 6 p.m. Most supervisors tell you the company policy on work sched-

ules and whether there is flexibility. Never be afraid to ask.

- Prepare for the upcoming week on the weekends or the night before for each day. This can involve picking out clothes, preparing to-go lunches, showering at night, etc. This can help you get out of the house quicker in the morning.

Managing Your Workload

Learn how to effectively manage your time. In most cases, you will be responsible for completing your tasks within a given timeframe. It is up to you to make sure you understand what you need to do to complete a requested task and when it is due. Sometimes you will have varying assignments you will need to complete with competing deadlines. It is up to you to prioritize the tasks and then get them done. The key to being efficient in managing multiple deadlines is to realize which tasks you can do quickly and which ones take time. Once you figure this out, you will be able to manage your day-to-day responsibilities with no problem. This skill will come with time so don't worry if there are a few bumps in the road along the way.

Another habit to adopt when it comes to time management is to alert your supervisor or task lead as soon as possible if you foresee any reason why you will not meet a given deadline. The earlier you make the higher ups aware of this, the sooner this is made clear and the easier it will be to find a solution to ensure the work gets done on time. Your boss may decide to extend your deadline or free you from other deadlines so that you can get your work done. Additional solutions your manager may present include: extending the deadline, freeing up your time from other work so you can focus on high priority tasks, assigning the work to another person, or providing you with additional clarification or assistance to help you complete the assignment. Another way to manage your workload is to get clarification on the task so that you can complete it. The worst thing you can do is wait until the deadline has arrived and then make it known that you have not completed your task. Part of managing your time also means focusing on your work. In this age of cell phones and tablets, it is easy to get distracted by text messages and social media sites. It is also easy to get carried away in hallway conversations or gossip. There is plenty of time for that during breaks and lunch time. Distractions during work hours can lead to late nights in the office finishing the work you could have done during the day.

If you have free time at work (downtime), you should spend it on activities that will help develop your career. This is an investment in your future. If you have a lot of availability, you should seek out new assignments. For short periods of downtime, consider taking training classes, reading articles or books related to your industry, increasing your expertise, or working on building relationships with coworkers. Learn more about your colleagues' jobs. Ask if you can help them in any way. Reach out to your supervisor to see what he or she recommends for you to do during your free time and obtain pre-approval for any of the activities mentioned here.

Work-life balance is another important issue to consider. When you first start a new job, it is easy to lose track of time and develop the habit of working extra hours. New employees do this to try to prove themselves. This is acceptable; however, realize that the late-nights and extra effort will be hard habits to break later. Working extra hours can conflict with your personal and social time. You will end up sacrificing time with your friends, family, and yourself. It is important not to get so wrapped up in your job that you don't take time for yourself. Working around-the-clock consistently over a long period of time can lead to burnout. You may even cause yourself physical or mental damage. Strokes, anxiety attacks, and stress can occur as a result of working too hard and/or too much. If you are an overachiever, you know how difficult it is to put yourself first and break the habit of doing extra work. The cold truth is that if you die today, work will go on tomorrow, so please don't put your health at risk. While it is important to do a good job at work, and that may mean working late sometimes, your mental and physical health should be a priority.

Some signs that you may be overworking yourself include:

1. You find that you are working late into the evening night after night.
2. No matter how hard you work at the to-do list, it keeps getting longer, and you constantly feel overwhelmed.
3. You are having trouble sleeping at night because you are thinking of all the things on your to-do list.
4. You lose track of time, meaning you feel like you blinked and two months passed.
5. Everyone is always telling you that you look tired.
6. You skip lunch at work and you rarely take breaks.
7. You get stress headaches or throbbing pains in the back of your neck.
8. Every day when you leave the office you tell yourself, 'I need a drink.'

Suggestions for Work-life Balance

1. Set a work schedule start and stop time, and stick to it.
2. Mentally turn off work when you leave the office. This takes practice and time, but if you stick with it, this will become easier to do.
3. Set appointments for after work. If you have somewhere to be after work that will reduce your likelihood of staying late.
4. Speak to your supervisor about delegating some of your work. It may be that you are trying to do the work of

two people and you need help. Don't be ashamed or embarrassed to ask for help. It's better to ask and get the help you need then to stress yourself out and have a heart attack.

5. Go to the gym. If you are feeling stressed or over whelmed as a result of work, physical activity can help relieve the tension in your muscles and help you relax.

6. Go to the spa. It's okay to treat yourself. If you have a job where you tense up or stress often, or work on computers all day, the spa is a great place to go and relax. Massages also help release tension in your muscles.

Following Company Policies

Companies establish policies and procedures to outline how business decisions and performance should occur in the workplace. Policies are developed to provide guidance at a high level on how work should be conducted, and procedures provide the framework for how policies should be applied to the work performed. There are various policies a company can put in place.

Some examples, along with their definitions, include the following:

- *Code of Ethics* – A high-level guideline that outlines acceptable behavior for what is 'right' and what is 'wrong' and how to apply these beliefs to the work that employees perform.

- *Social Media Policy* – A guideline for posting content on the Internet (and in some cases, the Intranet, a company's internal network) on behalf of the company or on individual social media outlets.
- *Dress Code Policy* – A set of rules that outline the acceptable attire for the workplace.

It is important to follow all company policies and procedures, including any additional guidance established by the segment of the company where you work. Not following company guidelines can set you up for disciplinary action including termination.

Etiquette

Etiquette in the workplace refers to how you behave and conduct yourself in a professional environment. Making the right decisions is important, but so is your posture (meaning the way you do things and the attitude you have when you do them). If you are asked to stay late one day to help finish a project that is running behind, it is easy to grumble. You may say "yes," and yet not mean it. Imagine the impression you'd have on your team if you complain the entire evening about missing your favorite TV shows. What you do and *how* you do it will develop the image people have of you. Do you want your coworkers to have a positive or negative perception of you? As a new hire, your goal should be to become the person everyone loves to work with, the one people can depend on. Most people would rather work with someone with a positive attitude who is friendly and a little less skilled than a person that is a top performer, but has a horrible attitude. In most cases, it is easier to help an employee develop a skill than to help them change their attitude and behavior. It is also important that you take constructive criticism well. If someone takes the time to point out ways that you can improve, listen and seek out ways to develop yourself. Don't take it personally. If someone were out to get you, have you fired, or make you look bad, he/she would not come to you and take the time to point out areas where you could improve.

Below is a list of behaviors and habits we have observed in the workplace that people often overlook:

1. Volume – It is a big no-no to talk so loud in the office environment that it disrupts a coworker's performance. It is common to make this mistake while taking personal calls at work or when socializing with coworkers in common areas. Be mindful of the people around you. You shouldn't talk so loudly that everyone around you knows exactly what your conversation is about.

2. Flirting – Your workplace is not Match.com. Openly flirting with coworkers is frowned upon in most work places. You do not want to say or do anything that can

make anyone you work with feel uncomfortable and report you to the Human Resources department. Don't put yourself at risk for sexual harassment or of being fired. Be sure to study your company's code of conduct to understand their policies on ethical and moral behavior.

3. Filter your speech – Aside from flirting, you should be careful not to say or do things that could offend others. This includes getting into religious or political debates at work. You should also refrain from other topics such as telling someone how they should or should not raise their children. A good way to avoid this is to stop before you speak and ask yourself, "Could what I am about to say be taken offensively?" If the answer is yes, don't even say it.

4. Personal hygiene and aromas – *Taking care of yourself is important as well. If you sit close to other people in the workplace, be sure you are taking care of your personal hygiene. Wouldn't you hate to sit next to someone who didn't believe in soap and water? There is also the other extreme. Some people can smell too good. Wearing an excessive amount of perfume or cologne can also be a distraction, especially for people with allergies. Be mindful of these things, especially when you have a work environment where you sit close to others.*

5. Personal space – Be considerate of other people's personal space. When talking to others, don't stand or sit so close that you are practically touching them. There should be enough space between you and the other person so that they don't have to worry about smelling your (bad) breath or feeling uncomfortable. This concept applies to your personal workspace as well. Some companies give their employees individual offices, some have cubicles, and others often have shared workspaces (workspaces rotated by various people). In each situation, you should keep your space neat and clean. There's nothing worse than taking home a bed bug you picked up at work or realizing that you are sitting in an ant pile while working, because the person who occupied the space before you left treats on the floor that attracted all kinds of creepy crawly guests. This also goes for public spaces other than your work space. When you use the restroom, be sure to clean up after yourself. No one wants to deal with your crap, literally. Also, if you have access to a shared kitchen, respect other people's food, beverages, and lunches. If you are starving and someone else's lunch in the refrigerator looks tempting, ask first before eating half of their sandwich. Yes, I (Christina) just said someone

could take your lunch. This has happened to poor little me several times. I guess that means I can cook! Be sure to clean up after yourself in the kitchen as well. Don't leave dirty containers and food scraps in or around the sink when you finish your lunch. Your company hired bright sharp employees, not maids.

Office Gossip

Don't be a talk show host at work. You don't want to be known as the person who can't keep a secret. This is the person where if they paid as much attention to their work as they did everyone's business they would be the CEO of the company. They know everyone's personal business, but can't even send a fax. Workplace gossip can get you into trouble, but it seems to be everywhere. Be careful about how you handle gossip that comes your way. If you are the one passing information along, you want to make sure of three things. First, be sure that the information you have is true. Second, ask yourself if you have the authority and permission to pass along the information, and third, ask yourself if you would be okay hearing it again from someone else. If you put it out there, you better be okay with everyone knowing it, because once it's out there, you can't take it back. It would be embarrassing to pass along gossip about someone being fired and then the next day they show up to work and you find out the conversation you overheard was not valid. You would look like an idiot for spreading a lie and you would have created an uncomfortable work environment for that employee. In addition, you would appear to be the office liar and your credibility would be questioned going forward. Bottom line, do not start gossiping and don't pass along the gossip that comes your way. If you hear anything that concerns you, like office closures or mass layoffs, then you should have a conversation with your supervisor to clear up any questions or worries you might have.

Dressing Appropriately

Dressing appropriately is exactly what it sounds like. Work is not the runway at New York Fashion Week, nor is it the club. In your first few weeks of working at a new company, you should dress to impress. If you are starting a new job and are not sure what to wear on the first day, think about how people were dressed when you interviewed, if in person. It's also a safe bet for a gentleman to wear a suit and tie and a lady to wear a pant or skirt suit. During the first few weeks, observe what others wear. Be sure to examine others in a position similar to yours and take note of what your coworkers wear Monday through Thursday and if they dress more casual on Fridays.

Most places have business professional dress codes Mondays through Thursdays with casual attire on Fridays. When in doubt, wear what the majority of your coworkers wear or dress like your supervisor. If he or she is in a suit every day, then you safely assume that it is okay to wear a suit every day. As time passes, you will get a sense of what works and what doesn't. As you make friends at work or find a mentor, you can ask for clarity on the dress code if you still don't have it down yet.

I (Christina) remember working with a young man in college who dressed to impress during his interview, but on his first day, he showed up in cargo shorts, a button up short sleeve shirt, and sandals. I remember thinking, "Is he going to the beach or coming to work?" Everyone else in the office was dressed business casual. The men wore slacks and polo tops or button-up long sleeve dress shirts, and the women wore office dresses, slacks and dress tops, or pant suits. As I got to know the young man, I learned that since he was a college intern, he didn't particularly care how he dressed. As a concerned coworker who understood the importance of an internship, I tried to explain to him that his position could land him a full-time job once he graduated. Even if he went somewhere else to work, he would need references, and employers sometimes consider references crucial in the hiring process. In my opinion, he had already set himself up for failure. He would have to be an amazing intern to counter the already negative perception he had portrayed. Dressing like he was at home relaxing created an image that he was lazy. This assumption turned out to be one hundred percent correct.

Lunch Time Do's and Don'ts

1. **Do not** dirty your work area. If you have the option of eating at your workstation, be neat. For example, don't eat powdered donuts and leave white powdered finger prints all over the keyboard. You do not want to be known as the person who brought in the ants and roaches. It is best to eat in a designated lunch area.

2. **Do not** bring in a dish that will smell up the entire office. Would you want to work all day in an office that smelled like cow dung?

3. **Do not** take extended lunches. Stick to your given time allowance for lunch. If your supervisor cannot trust you to return from lunch on time, how would he/she trust you with a task that could cost the company money? Extended lunch breaks also speak negatively to your time management skills. If you need to take a long lunch, possibly to run a necessary errand, give your supervisor a heads up. Likewise, you may need to stay longer to make up the time.

4. **Do** use lunchtime as your personal time. Lunchtime is the perfect time to conduct any personal business. For example, make personal phone calls on your own phone

or run errands. Just make sure you conduct your personal business in the allowed timeslot or the time that your supervisor has pre-approved.

5. **Do** take a lunch break. It's easy to get carried away working and work through lunch. It is important that you take lunch to get a mental break and step away for a moment. There may be a time or two where your workload is heavy and you need to use your lunch break to get ahead, but if you do this often, it's a problem. Skipping meals is not good for your health. It is an indicator of stress and possibly an indicator of a bigger problem.

Emails

Some companies and/or positions do not allow access to the Internet in the workplace. That makes it easy not to check or send personal emails. In other positions, where there is access to the Internet, it can be challenging not to quickly check or send personal emails. A key point to remember is if you do not want your supervisor to read the email out loud to the company, then do not send it. Once you send your message from a company device, anyone can retrieve it and read it. Yes, work emails can be hacked. Be careful what you send through your company's email and instant messaging applications. In today's workplace, everything is tracked and can be pulled up at any time. You should not be on personal email on your work computer during work hours. This too can be tracked and can be used to terminate you if your usage violates your workplace code of conduct. Be sure to read your company policy on security and understand what is permitted.

Sharing Your Personal Business

You may have enjoyed your trip to the beach and thought you looked cute in your two-piece bikini or speedo, but you don't need to come to work and show everyone a picture of it. Be careful what personal business you share in the workplace. Do not have your friends and lovers meet you in the lobby or outside in the parking lot if you have drama. You don't want that to spill over into the workplace and make you look bad. For example, you're sitting in your car before coming into the office and you're on the phone fighting with your boyfriend/girlfriend. You are yelling loudly and cursing. Someone pulls up into the parking space next to you and you don't even notice because you are in a heated argument. Note, the work parking lot is considered a part of the office and how you carry yourself at all times can be used against you. Back to the example...Finally, you hang up the phone and you look over to your left at the car that pulled up next to you, and sitting inside the car is the CEO of your company. That is not a good look.

There is a time and place to disclose personal information. Some examples of when it is acceptable to share personal business in the office would be during lunch time, special holidays, and office gatherings that encourage socializing. Bring a kid to work day, with approval of course, is a great time to brag about your kids. Sharing celebratory news of events like a wedding or baby can be exciting, especially when cake is involved. Holiday parties and gatherings that you will attend by yourself or with guests are appropriate venues to discuss hobbies and activities that you are involved in outside of work in an attempt to network and connect with coworkers. All of these are good examples of when sharing personal news with others in the workplace would be appropriate. Sharing your business is inappropriate when it could make others feel uncomfortable or cause offense. Disclosing information about your indigestion issues over lunch while others are eating would be inappropriate. Discussing your latest sexual conquest at the water cooler near other coworkers would also be inappropriate. Sending out a company email to solicit funds for a local politician you really believe in is totally inappropriate. When in doubt, don't do it.

Company Events

People often say, "I am not going to any work events after work hours. I am not getting paid for that." As you are trying to build your career and advance to the next level, it is important to network. One of the unwritten rules to advancement in the work place is networking outside of work hours. Company events, such as office holiday parties and company picnics, are other ways for you to meet key players within your organization and learn the 'stories' of others. It also provides you an opportunity to introduce yourself to people you wouldn't otherwise interact with. You never know who you might meet, so look at these events as opportunities to gain exposure and meet your coworkers. Sometimes it is WHO you know, not WHAT you know that will help you get ahead. The same goes for gatherings during the workday. Sacrificing a few minutes to attend someone's wedding, birthday, or baby celebration won't kill you and these are chances to meet people and introduce yourself. You also show yourself to be personable and you get to practice your soft skills (people, social, communication skills, etc.). You could be the brightest person within your organization with lots of great ideas, but no one would ever know it if you just stayed at your desk and performed your daily tasks without ever talking to anyone.

Oh Raine. We get it, sometimes you need a few snacks to stay awake and get that extra energy you need to keep going at work, but this is ridiculous. It is important to keep your work space clean and organized. You will be more successful this way. Raine probably reminds you of someone in your office, just don't let it be you.

Chapter 3
Developing Yourself Like a BOSS

If you have already landed your dream job, you may be asking yourself *how do I get a promotion*? Perhaps you have been in the same role at work for a while and you want more responsibility. What do you do? How do let your boss know that you are ready for the next level? Do you know if you are ready for that next level?

Developing yourself plays a huge part in workplace advancement, but exactly how to do that isn't always crystal clear. First, you have to recognize the areas where you need improvement, and second, figure out how to go about getting the development you need. Sometimes you need someone else's perspective to help you identify the things you do well in addition to the areas where you may need improvement. In this section, we're going to provide tips on how to position yourself for growth and build strategic relationships that will assist you in doing so.

Identifying Your Options

Once you find yourself in a new work environment, whether it is your first career job or a change in companies, you should identify a career path that you would like to see yourself on. This includes talking to other employees, asking questions, gathering information, and attending company events. Try to identify who's who within the company. Once you have a handle on all the different job titles, you can think about which office or position you would like to have. Once you do this, all you need is a strategy for achieving your goal. For example, if you are a teacher and you start teaching math at an all girls' high school, your dream of becoming a boy's wrestling coach is not likely to happen. If you realize that what you really desire to do is not an option at your current workplace, you have two options to consider. One, talk to your supervisor about the possibility of creating a new opportunity. If this is something encouraged in your workplace, you may get the chance to pioneer the new position. If this is not an option in your workplace, don't be afraid to leave and seek opportunities elsewhere. If you plan on working for the next twenty years, then you should be doing something you like. If you identify a position or career path within your current workplace that interests you, it would be a good idea to talk with the person(s) in this role. You could suggest lunch or a meeting to allow that person to talk about their role and how they achieved it. You should also let your supervisor know your career goals so that they will have a clear picture of what you want and can help find you opportunities to grow in that area.

Developing Relationships

Various sources indicate that approximately sixty percent of jobs or more are obtained through networking, and many people secure their dream positions based on referrals. Networking is the process of continually developing and sustaining mutually beneficial relationships.

The purposes of networking are to:

1. Build relationships – The people who you meet are key to your success. Perhaps they have insight on a position that you are curious about or they started off where you are and have worked their way up in the company. As a result, they are invaluable and can help you to connect with other like-minded individuals or provide you with steps to navigate the workplace.

2. Learn new skills – When you network, you are likely to encounter new ways of doing things. Stay open-minded. Increasing your skills will allow you to become more valuable and marketable for other positions and opportunities.

3. Increase visibility – Networking opens the doors to meeting new people. Let's say you talk with someone about a specific skill set that you have or a project you completed. It just so happens that this person is looking for someone with your skill set and calls you a week later to see if you would be interested in taking on a new project, position, etc. You would never have been approached regarding this new opportunity if you had not been networking.

4. Share knowledge – Many companies have mentoring initiatives or employee-related clubs that meet frequently to discuss various issues including workplace success. When you are a part of one of these, it is important to take advantage of any opportunities to share ideas with your group and to lead sessions when applicable. This is yet another opportunity to increase your visibility while sharing more about what you know, what you are doing, and what you would like to do.

Types of networking include social (i.e. friends, family, volunteers, and neighbors) and professional/business, which occurs in the workplace, or through committee involvement, chambers of commerce, networking events, and small business development groups. Nowadays, even social media can assist with networking and getting to know others; however, you want to be careful what kind of information you are putting out into cyber-space about yourself. Companies like hiring people that are referred by current employees. For example, if you are looking to network with someone who is employed with a specific organi-zation, you could use the LinkedIn site to search for that organi-zation and then ask to connect with individuals of your choosing. Most companies view referrals as less risky because they are more likely to stay with the company, whereas applicants who are not referred are viewed as flight risks (people who may leave the com-pany).

Some tips for networking include:

- knowing yourself
- knowing the purpose of why you want to network
- joining organizations
- asking for referrals
- attending job fairs
- sending thank-you notes after meeting people
- attending industry-related conferences for your line of work

As you are making a name for yourself, it is important to network and make yourself known. If the CEO of a company is looking to promote employees with project management skills and you are certified as a Project Management Professional (PMP) and nobody knows that, then you've just missed out on an opportunity. You need to develop healthy relationships with your co-workers. The more people who know your name and your skill set, the more your name will be mentioned when opportunities arise. So be sure to work *and* network, and in doing so, brag a little. However, do not talk about things you cannot do because that can harm you, but it is okay to mention certifications you have obtained and other skills and abilities that you consider as your strengths. Remember the key words are brag *a little.* No one likes a know-it-all.

What's a Mentor?

We have all reached that pivotal moment when we just don't know what to do, where to start, who to talk to, what to ask, and so on. For me (Camille), it was a matter of life (an optimistic moment of opportunity) and death (a conscious decision to give up). So, I sought out a mentor.

A mentor is:

- someone who acts as a guide
- an advisor
- a counselor
- a coach
- a person who makes you reflect on your strengths and weaknesses
- someone who challenges you to become a better version of yourself

- flexible and considers what type of relationship best suits you
- someone who sets boundaries
- an individual you can trust
- one who can provide you with feedback and constructive criticism
- a compass, as they can help you navigate challenges successfully

A mentor is not:

- a dictator
- a person to vent to about all of your job dislikes
- always a person in a higher position
- someone who has the same challenges as you
- peer

A mentoring relationship can be:

- formal with a set objectives and frequent meeting times laid out on a schedule
- informal, with discussions about current challenges and unscheduled meetings

I (Camille) have had mentors at work for professional development and outside of work for my own personal growth. For my personal growth, I found someone who had great qualities and posed the question, "would you mind being my mentor?" I further added, "You portray a lot of the qualities that I am aiming for both personally and professionally." Voila! A mentorship was born! I felt like I hit the mentor jackpot! We established a date for our first meeting. I knew I had a great mentor when, during our first meeting, she asked me what I hoped to accomplish by meeting with her and how often I would like to meet. My first homework assignment was to develop a plan that included my strengths and weaknesses, and areas that I wanted to focus on improving. A mentor that provided homework…how EXCELLENT! You may be wondering why I was so excited. Well, it's because she was challenging me, and you need someone in your space that is going to do just that. Where challenge meets action, you experience growth.

Personal SWOT Analysis

I (Camille) searched for a viable online template that would help me to showcase my current strengths and weaknesses. I ended up coming across what is referred to in the business world as a SWOT Analysis.

You may or may not have heard about SWOT Analysis. SWOT is an acronym for Strengths, Weaknesses, Opportunities, and Threats. Does this sound intimidating? It's really not. When SWOT is applied to corporations, it is generally used as part of strategic planning processes to gauge internal strengths and weaknesses in relation to external opportunities and threats. Another way to put it is a process of determining where the organization is currently, where it wants to go, the propellers that will help to expedite the journey ahead, the anchors that can keep it stuck in place, and the icebergs that will prevent it from getting there. You can apply this same concept to your individual performance at work. Every company participates in some form of employee performance review. They are usually conducted annually. You can use the SWOT analysis method to track your growth from year-to-year. It is beneficial to know your strengths and weaknesses. You should do this at least annually prior to your review so that you can measure your growth. After identifying your strengths and weaknesses, write out a plan for how you will improve in both areas, including opportunities that you will seek out such as trainings, certifications, and classes, deadlines for all the items and action steps you plan to pursue in order to complete all of your tasks. You should review this regularly throughout the year to ensure that you are staying on track with your plan. It's a great idea to ask for advice from a mentor or supervisor on how you can improve and to ask them for other yearly goal suggestions that you should set for yourself.

Refer to the workbook for additional details on SWOT analysis and for a sample template you can use to determine your strengths, weaknesses, opportunities, and threats.

Workplace Brand

If you are just starting out in your industry, then you have to make a name for yourself. Think of this as creating a *brand* for yourself. Another way to think of this is 'when people hear my name, what is the first thing that comes to mind?' It is important to know your strengths *and* weaknesses. When you begin to think about (and create) your workplace brand, focus on your strengths, what you do well. The goal of branding yourself is to inspire people to think positively about you. The way to do this is to put in extra effort, work a little later than usual, do more than what is requested, take initiative (instead of waiting to be told what to do), and help others even if you don't receive credit. All of these things go into building your brand at work, as well as producing quality work. If you are required to produce a spreadsheet, memo, product, or anything else, it has your name on it. You want to make sure that you produce quality work. You never know who is going to see the fruits of your labor. Treat every task you work on like it is the difference between having a job and not having one. Once you have made a name for yourself, you can back off on working the extra hours and trying so hard to please. You may still have to grind from time-to-time but not as often. You may not notice your extra efforts paying off in the beginning. It may take six months or six years, but it will definitely pay off. These initial periods help us figure out things about ourselves as well. You may learn that you don't really like this job—what you thought you wanted to do, forty hours a week fifty-two weeks a year—as much as you thought you would. You might even be introduced to something new that you find a passion for.

Here are some personal branding questions to consider:

1. What is your professional mission?
2. Who is your professional audience?
3. What are three words that OTHER PEOPLE use to describe you?
4. Would you change anything about your appearance? Be honest with yourself. Does your hair, work attire, etc., contribute to a positive personal brand?
5. What are some things you can improve about your verbal and non-verbal communication? Are you a good listener? Do you use words like, "um" too much? Is it difficult to keep eye contact? Do you smile often, or no?
6. Are there any skills that you need to develop further, such as presenting, speaking, or time management?
7. Do you get involved in company initiatives?
8. Would you hire you?
9. Do you help others *with a positive attitude*?

Corporate and External Training

It can be hard to keep up with the growing pace of technology and the constant wave of new concepts and various complexities of industries nowadays. As people who have worked in several different industries (i.e. retail, telemarketing, financial, communications, data analytics, and more). We can certainly attest to feeling behind the curve at times. However, we're here to tell you that there are ways in which you can stay on top of pressing issues, trends, and other changes that affect your career path. More companies now realize the need to train their employees in order for them to gain skills for current or future positions. As a result, employees can turn to their own training and development departments (often linked to the human resources division of a company) to gain new skills. Many organizations facilitate assessments that provide insight on employees' current skill levels and how they match up with various positions within the company. This is a great benefit to have, and it also indicates that the company believes employees are their most valuable resources. Job rotation is another internal source of building on your skill set. According to the dictionary by Merriam-Webster, "job rotation" *is the assigning of an employee to a variety of tasks in turn to provide diversified experience during training or to counteract boredom.* Continuous learning can be very valuable in your future endeavors or in solidifying your longevity with the company. Seek external training opportunities when your company does not have such programs. You may want to gain professional recognition by obtaining a certification to showcase your expertise. For example, an accountant may choose to set themselves apart by obtaining a Certified Professional Accountant (CPA) designation or an engineer may do so by obtaining a Professional Engineer (PE) designation. Another external platform for developing yourself is to take continuing education classes at a local community college or from another established source.

Whether you identify internal or external development opportunities, keep in mind that it is up to you to take the time to develop yourself. Try setting aside a certain night each week as your professional development time. This will allow you a chance to catch up on emerging trends and issues, take online training classes offered by your employer to gain insight on topics you're not familiar with, and to read various books. Part of your development time may even include reading up on various things you plan to do in the future. As we mentioned earlier, filling out a personal SWOT Analysis will allow you to target the personal and professional development areas you want to focus on so that you can excel in the workplace.

Anytime you can learn something new or increase your existing level of understanding, you should take advantage of it. In today's society with all the advances in technology, things are constantly changing. You can't expect that what you learned a couple of years ago to still be applicable five years from now. As time changes, so must you. Investing time in yourself is well worth it as it will help you grow and develop. Once you feel you have mastered a certain area, you can offer training to others, thus improving upon your workplace brand. Therefore, go ahead and give up an hour of television every night for a few months. You can always watch your favorite shows later On Demand thanks to technology.

Help, I'm Stuck! (What do you do when you don't know what to do?)

You may find yourself in a position when you are asked to do something that you don't know how to do. In this situation, you have two options. First, tell the requestor, "I don't know how to do that. Can you provide me with some additional direction?" Second, figure it out. The first option will work a couple of times depending on how new you are in your position (that is, your level in the company and the position you have). One indicator that an employee is ready for a promotion is that they do not ask for instructions every time they are given a task. Having said that, please do not struggle quietly for hours because you don't want to appear like you don't know what you are doing.

If you choose to take the second option and try to figure it out on your own, here are some tips. First, seek advice from your mentor or someone more senior (than you) whom you trust. They might understand the task more clearly and can provide you with additional guidance. Second, search for information via the Internet, using search engines like Google, for processes and terminology you need explained. Google helps! If something similar has been done, try looking at other examples to see if those examples add any clarification. Warning, if you choose to figure a task out on your own, do not spend too much time doing so. If you have spent an entire day trying to figure something out and you have no luck and the requestor wanted results an hour after they spoke with you, there's a problem!

You have to gauge how much time you are going to give yourself to figure something out on your own. Consider when the task needs to be complete and if you have available resources from which to glean. Otherwise, asking up front for clarification or help is perfectly okay. Sometimes, there may be tasks that nobody in your office will know how to do, but because of who you are and the workplace brand you have made for yourself, you will be asked to complete them. Although it may seem overwhelming and impossible, keep a positive attitude, trust in your abilities, and do what you do best. There is a reason you were selected to work on that task. When you first start out in a new position, it may seem like you are always looking stuff up on Google, asking for additional guidance, or searching resource manuals. This is okay. As time goes on, you will begin to pick up on things and you won't need to do as much research. Your job will become second-nature. School does not teach us exactly what we will face in the real world. It just teaches us the basics of what we need to get a job done. It is our job to make the connection between what we are being asked to do and which skills we can use to get it done. A good analogy would be that school teaches us what eggs, milk, flour, sugar, bowls, spoons, ovens, kitchens, and time are, but it is up to us to go into the kitchen and make a cake.

Raine planned to commit herself to self-development. She had the right idea, but she's easily distracted. Putting in extra effort to get ahead will require self-discipline. The question is, how bad do you want that promotion?

Chapter 4
What Are You Saying About Yourself?

What you say and who you say it to will help shape or harm your professional career. Communication goes along with the "Workplace Habits" chapter. Both of these topics are about the way others in your company perceive you. In other words, their perceptions are developed by what you do and how you do it.

External Social Media

You may have heard the saying "you are the company you keep." It is important to represent yourself well within and outside of the workplace. We can recall several instances when we searched through various posts on Facebook and had that thought. If you think you are going to get a job working for a large corporate giant and you are constantly posting about how drunk you are at your weekend party events, then think again! This behavior reflects your character! Posting tasteless photos or images that compromise your integrity and everything you thought you stood for when it comes to the workplace are not worth posting. If you have social media sites that you frequently post to and your posts are vulgar or offensive, you should make your accounts private to limit the number of people who can access them. If you want to leave your social media accounts public, make sure you are not posting anything that can be offensive to anyone or anything that represents your company in a negative way. For example, if you worked at a doctor's office and someone you don't like comes in for a visit, don't look up their file and post their medical condition on Facebook. It's also not wise to tweet or post statuses about customers, clients, coworkers or supervisors, even if you aren't identifying these people by name. It is tasteless and can create a negative of image of you to current or future colleagues.

Nowadays, with social media on the rise, trends towards this avenue for acquiring new talent are also heightened. More and more employers review social media outlets prior to inviting potential employees to interview. Companies also use social media to help share their company culture with others, market products, and create brands. As mentioned in the interview section, recruiters are checking social media pages regularly. What do your social media sites say about you? Once hired, you represent the company you work for. If a post is questionable, don't post it! Just know that anything placed on the Internet stays on the Internet. In addition to using social media and avoiding posting the wrong things, you should also avoid posting comments on controversial topics like politics. These are also topics you shouldn't be talking about in the workplace. You do not want to make your employer and/or your colleagues feel uncomfortable. Perhaps your way of expressing yourself is by hanging posters or other items that represent you. Posting items in your workplace that are indicative of political or social views is probably not something you should do. For example, a poster that says, "Kill Them All," is probably not a good idea even if it is just a quote from your favorite movie. Someone in the office could misinterpret you and/or your intentions and create a pretty upsetting road ahead for you that potentially ends in job loss. Just avoid it all together.

Check your company handbook and familiarize yourself with company policy (and unwritten culture) on using company resources, such as the computer and Internet, to check your social media. It would be senseless to get fired for getting on your Facebook page at work to post about how much you loved your lunch when you could have waited until you got home to do that or just used your own personal phone.

Work-Related Social Skills

Social skills are the way you communicate and interact with others. Your social skills can label you positively or negatively by others. Good social skills can help you build strong relationships, lead to effective teamwork, and increase your opportunity for advancement. Don't find yourself spiraling down the wrong path and becoming 'Cameron, the Complainer'. I (Camille) have found myself in situations where I was filled with workplace complaints and other frustrations. In the past, this was an indicator for evaluating whether or not it was time to find a new job or to change my perspective of the current one. Of course, the latter is a great option that we should always implement; however, it's not always the easiest to do. Changing jobs is fine, but if you don't create a new way to deal with work frustrations and complaints, the pattern will continue and you will always find yourself switching jobs. You might want to try venting to your close friends or family members, who are not affiliated with your place of employment.

There's yet another person, 'Chatty Cathy', who has a habit of talking to everyone and telling her life story, which can be distracting to others who are trying to do their work. A simple solution is to let this person know that you have something to finish up by a certain timeframe so you can't talk right now. You can even let her (or him) know that you're willing to talk with them later over lunch. Last, but not least, let's chime in on 'Debbie Downer'. Perhaps you've seen the countless *Saturday Night Live* clips on this character. If not, you should check them out. Debbie Downer has a habit of seeing the glass as half empty all the time and suck-ing the life out of the party. It's as if the words "fun" and "happy" were erased from this person's brain and replaced with misery and sadness. Don't be this person! No one (in their right mind) will want to be around you. People like to be around people that are genuine, have their best interests in mind, and follow through on what they say. People love optimistic individuals who speak life, not doom.

Some people think that work is simply getting a job, work-ing at their desk all day, and going home when the day is over. Why do they need social skills in the workplace? There are many benefits to having good communication and social skills in the workplace.

- First of all, people like working with other people who communicate effectively. In a work environment where there are teams of people, it is good if you can read peo-ple and interact with different personalities and cultures.
- Secondly, effective communication creates opportunities to represent the company publicly. If you are someone who can communicate clearly and effectively, you may be asked to attend meetings where clients or upper management will be present. Your approachability and ability to read people and adapt in social settings also become valuable in various professional environments,

such as conferences, seminars, or cross-departmental meetings.

- Third, the ability to communicate complex topics in a simplistic manner opens the doors to create and lead trainings, and other opportunities to demonstrate your effectiveness with communicating in the workplace. These opportunities may position you in front of key individuals who can make decisions in your favor leading to potential promotion opportunities.Saying, "It's time for my promotion!" on day one is not realistic. If receiving a promotion is a motivating factor for you, great! However, an appropriate approach to making this known would be to have strategic conversations over time with your direct supervisor or manager on a regular basis (perhaps monthly), and possibly with their leader (i.e. director, vice president, etc.) on a less frequent basis (that is, quarterly). It is great that you are ambitious and know what goals you want to achieve, but sharing your goals with your supervisor may help you achieve them sooner. Remember, timing is everything. Be sure you have a proven track record before requesting a promotion.

- Lastly, effective social skills can also open the doorway to supervising roles. People who can communicate well with others make for good supervisors and mentors. This is why the "Development" chapter is so important as you should know your strengths and your weaknesses.

Be Careful What You Say and Who You Say It To

"Uh oh! I didn't know that lady was the boss' niece. Aaaaaaaaaaaaaaaaaahhhhhhhhhhhhh!" Don't let this be you! Be aware of your surroundings always. In addition, don't have hallway discussions that someone else may overhear and misinterpret. Step away from your desk when you take personal calls and go to a secluded area, if possible. It is okay to return a missed call during your lunch break, but you may want to consider going outside or to your vehicle when you do so, depending on how your workplace is set up. Let me reiterate, you don't want to talk to someone and find out later that they are best friends or the golfing buddy of the person you were talking to them about. Be mindful of these types of things, and like we mentioned earlier, do not use your peers or others as your outlet for venting. Establish this type of connection with someone outside of the workplace and make sure that they have no ties to anyone in the company. If you want to be even more careful, use general scenarios when you vent so that the person you speak with cannot easily identify a single individual or situation.

What does the phrase "office politics" refer to? According

to Wikipedia, "It is the use of power and social networking within an organization to achieve changes that benefit the organization or individuals within it." When you first start a job, you are in a new environment, and like a poker player in a new casino, you must learn the house rules before you can maximize your wins. The best way to do this is to observe things for a while. Get to know your coworkers. Learn who talks too much and who doesn't talk enough. Identify who gets ahead and how they do it. This comes with time. You must also decide if you like the environment and if you want to remain and grow there. If you decide to move on to another opportunity with a more ideal environment, that is okay. Be sure to remain professional as you transfer or resign so that you do not burn any bridges. You may decide one day that you want to return to the company or you may need a reference from them for your future endeavors. If you decide to stay, then it is time to identify the career path you want and build a strategy on how to accomplish your goals. This goes hand-in-hand with networking and finding a mentor, because he or she would be able to help you learn the 'office politics' in your workplace. Your growth in the company depends on you not only being a sharp employee who is on top of your game, but also understanding your company culture and how its employees operate. That's right, you should show up to work on time, be dependable, prove that you are intelligent and savvy, and know who to talk to when you need something and who to avoid. These are unwritten rules that will help you climb the corporate ladder faster.

You should also watch what you say and do and how you say and do it. You have to be 'on' at all times. Think of it like this: someone is watching you always; never allow yourself to get so relaxed that you begin to arrive late, spend all day online shopping, fail to learn new skills, or become complacent with your job. I remember when I (Christina) started a new position with a relatively small company. I went in every morning around the same time, and on my way in, I would often pass a coworker who would always say, "Good morning Christina." I would smile and reply, "Good morning," and continue to my desk. I would think to myself *who is this man and how does he know my name.* About a year later, I learned he was the vice president. Once I found out who he was I thought *I am so glad I always smiled and replied good morning back.* What if I would have ignored him because I didn't know him or care who he was or was too busy texting or checking my social media? People in your office will know you before you know them. You want it to be for the right reasons: your pleasant smile, your optimistic attitude, or your can-do personality. Office politics, to some, may seem silly or irrelevant, and although it is possible to succeed in the workplace without them, understanding office politics can help you accelerate your success.

Although selfies are great and really capture the essence of who you are, you may not want to post them all on your social media accounts. This image doesn't exactly say "Young Successful Professional." What do your social media profiles say about you?

Chapter 5
Where's My Money?

DISCLAIMER: The information in this section is meant to help you understand the difference between your gross and net pay. In other words, this means the amount of money you negotiated at the time of hire versus the actual amount that you receive on payday. Any recommendations we make are solely recommendations based on our personal experiences. In understanding all the details of your paystub, you should consult your Human Resources department, and regarding your savings needs, you should consult a financial advisor.

It's here! It's here! Your first paycheck has arrived! You race to open the envelope to review your paystub or perhaps you electronically view it at work. You think to yourself, *what are all these deductions* (i.e. subtractions) *coming out of my check? I did not sign up for these.* Well, actually *you* did. Do you recall filling out oodles of employment forms with Human Resources (HR), including the Form W-4 Employee's Withholding Allowance

Certificate? If not, we guarantee you did. This document was established by the Internal Revenue Service (IRS), the government agency responsible for tax collection and tax law enforcement, as a way to help employers know how much federal income tax to reserve from employees' paychecks. Most employees are not exempt from paying federal income taxes. This worksheet comes with a guideline that will help you determine the number of exemptions you are allowed to claim. We include an excerpt of the bottom portion of this form for illustration purposes only.

Source: www.irs.gov

If you claim zero exemptions, the maximum amount of federal income taxes for your filing status (see #3 on the form above) will be calculated by your employer and subtracted from your pay. The more exemptions you have, the more pay you will take home as your employer will withhold less federal income taxes from your pay. This form is generally not provided to workers who will be independent contractors. Refer to the "Employee vs. Independent Contractor" section below for additional details on recognized employment classifications.

Employee vs. Independent Contractor

How you are treated on the job is important! No, I'm not talking about how you yourself are treated personally. Instead, I (Camille) am referring to how you are paid and the effect it can have on your taxable income and/or business deductions. If you are treated as an **employee** by your employer, then your employer is responsible for withholding income taxes, Social Security, and Medicare taxes; and paying unemployment taxes on wages paid to you. On the flip side, if you are treated as an **independent contractor** by your employer, then you are responsible for tracking your income and expenses related to work you perform and for paying federal income taxes. The IRS considers independent contractors to be self-employed individuals who perform services that cannot be controlled by an employer (that is, the employer does not have a say in what work is performed or how the work will be performed). As a self-employed person, you should receive a Form 1099-MISC "Miscellaneous Income" from the company you work for, especially if you have been paid $600 or more for work you performed. For additional details on what you are responsible for and your rights as an independent contractor, refer to the IRS's website at www.irs.gov.

Hourly versus Salary

You may be wondering what the difference is between being an hourly employee versus a salaried employee. For starters, an hourly employee is someone who receives a set amount of pay for each hour worked, whereas a salaried employee receives an agreed upon amount of pay per year no matter how many hours he or she works. Let's review the following scenarios for both an hourly employee and a salaried employee.

Scenario 1 – Denton worked forty hours a week at $20 an hour and is paid bi-weekly. By multiplying $20 an hour by the number of hours worked for one week, the total amount of pay for one week of work is $800. Since Denton is paid bi-weekly, he has made a gross profit of $1,600 ($800 per week multiplied by two weeks) for the pay period.

86

Scenario 2 – Kenya is paid an annual salary of $50,000 and is also paid bi-weekly. To calculate Kenya's pay for the pay period, we need to take Kenya's annual salary and divide it by the number of pay periods in the year. This equates to $1,923.08 ($50,000 ÷ 26 bi-weekly pay periods). This is Kenya's bi-weekly gross profit. Kenya's hourly amount can be found by dividing $1,923.08 by 80 (40 hours a week multiplied by 2 weeks) hours to arrive at $24.04 per hour. The amount is the same even if Kenya works extra hours during the week (more than 40) because she is paid salary.

Employees who are paid on an hourly basis are generally subject to receiving overtime pay (which means pay at one and a half times the hourly rate (1.5 times)) for hours worked in excess of forty hours in a week. The work week (and or number of hours considered to be a regular work week) does not have to follow a set guideline. For example, fifty hours may be considered the normal work week and the work week may be Friday through Thursday versus Monday through Friday. Be sure to review the human resources policies for your job so that you are aware of these details. Below is a scenario that illustrates overtime pay.

Scenario 3 – Denton worked ninety hours this pay period consisting of forty-two hours for week one and forty-eight hours for week two. The work week is Monday through Friday and is based on a forty-hour work week. Using the amounts from Scenario 1, we can calculate Denton's pay as follows:

Week 1 = ($20 per hour x 40 hours) + [($20 per hour x 1.5) x 2 hours]

$$= (\$800) + [(\$30) \times 2]$$
$$= (\$800) + [60]$$
$$= \$860$$

Week 2 = ($20 per hour x 40 hours) + [($20 per hour x 1.5) x 8 hours]

$$= (\$800) + [(\$30) \times 8]$$
$$= (\$800) + [\$240]$$
$$= \$1,040$$

Total pay for the two weeks equals $1,900 ($860 for Week 1 plus $1,040 for Week 2).

Salaried employees typically do not receive overtime. Make sure you are aware of your company's policies regarding your status as either an hourly or salaried employee.

Understanding Your Paycheck

Alright, now that we have that established, let's dig in to the actual paycheck! If you didn't have the opportunity to take a personal finance class in high school or college, or to learn from a savvy family member, a (personal) check is a piece of paper that allows the owner of a bank account to pay funds to another person or a business entity without having to exchange actual money. Basically, the check is a representation of funds. A company paycheck is a check provided to an employee or independent contractor for hourly wages or a defined salary amount. Paychecks are typically provided to employees on a bi-weekly basis; however, your employer can establish less or more frequent distribution periods.

Nowadays, most companies pay their employees through direct deposit, which eliminates the need to print out and provide paper checks. In this case, instead of receiving a paper check, you will receive a pay stub.

A pay stub generally consists of the following:

1. Employer's name
2. Employee's name
3. The last four digits of the employee's social security number
4. Pay period – the date range applicable for payment
5. Filing status for federal income tax – for example, Single, Married, Head of Household
6. Number of withholdings for federal and state taxes, if applicable, social security, and Medicare

Form **1040EZ**	Department of the Treasury—Internal Revenue Service **Income Tax Return for Single and Joint Filers With No Dependents** (99)	**2016**	OMB No. 1545-0074

Your first name and initial	Last name		Your social security number
If a joint return, spouse's first name and initial	Last name		Spouse's social security number
Home address (number and street). If you have a P.O. box, see instructions.		Apt. no.	▲ Make sure the SSN(s) above are correct.
City, town or post office, state, and ZIP code. If you have a foreign address, also complete spaces below (see instructions).			**Presidential Election Campaign** Check here if you, or your spouse if filing jointly, want $3 to go to this fund. Checking a box below will not change your tax or refund. ☐ You ☐ Spouse
Foreign country name	Foreign province/state/county	Foreign postal code	

Income

Attach Form(s) W-2 here.

Enclose, but do not attach, any payment.

1 Wages, salaries, and tips. This should be shown in box 1 of your Form(s) W-2.
   Attach your Form(s) W-2. .... **1**

2 Taxable interest. If the total is over $1,500, you cannot use Form 1040EZ. **2**

3 Unemployment compensation and Alaska Permanent Fund dividends (see instructions). **3**

4 Add lines 1, 2, and 3. This is your **adjusted gross income**. **4**

5 If someone can claim you (or your spouse if a joint return) as a dependent, check
   the applicable box(es) below and enter the amount from the worksheet on back.
   ☐ You   ☐ Spouse
   If no one can claim you (or your spouse if a joint return), enter $10,350 if **single**;
   $20,700 if **married filing jointly**. See back for explanation. **5**

6 Subtract line 5 from line 4. If line 5 is larger than line 4, enter -0-.
   This is your **taxable income**. .... ▶ **6**

Payments, Credits, and Tax

7 Federal income tax withheld from Form(s) W-2 and 1099. .... **7**

8a Earned income credit (EIC) (see instructions) **8a**

 b Nontaxable combat pay election. **8b**

9 Add lines 7 and 8a. These are your **total payments and credits**. .... ▶ **9**

10 Tax. Use the amount on **line 6 above** to find your tax in the tax table in the
    instructions. Then, enter the tax from the table on this line. **10**

11 Health care: individual responsibility (see instructions)   Full-year coverage ☐ **11**

12 Add lines 10 and 11. This is your **total tax**. **12**

Refund

Have it directly deposited! See instructions and fill in 13b, 13c, and 13d, or Form 8888.

13a If line 9 is larger than line 12, subtract line 12 from line 9. This is your **refund**.
     If Form 8888 is attached, check here ▶ ☐ **13a**

 ▶ b Routing number [ ] [ ] [ ] [ ] [ ] [ ] [ ] [ ] [ ]   ▶ c Type: ☐ Checking ☐ Savings

 ▶ d Account number [ ] [ ] [ ] [ ] [ ] [ ] [ ] [ ] [ ] [ ] [ ] [ ] [ ] [ ] [ ] [ ] [ ]

Amount You Owe

14 If line 12 is larger than line 9, subtract line 9 from line 12. This is
    the amount you owe. For details on how to pay, see instructions. .... ▶ **14**

Third Party Designee

Do you want to allow another person to discuss this return with the IRS (see instructions)? ☐ **Yes. Complete below.** ☐ No

Designee's name ▶ | Phone no. ▶ | Personal identification number (PIN) ▶

Sign Here

Joint return? See instructions.

Keep a copy for your records.

Under penalties of perjury, I declare that I have examined this return and, to the best of my knowledge and belief, it is true, correct, and accurately lists all amounts and sources of income I received during the tax year. Declaration of preparer (other than the taxpayer) is based on all information of which the preparer has any knowledge.

Your signature	Date	Your occupation	Daytime phone number
Spouse's signature. If a joint return, both must sign.	Date	Spouse's occupation	If the IRS sent you an Identity Protection PIN, enter it here (see inst.)

Paid Preparer Use Only

Print/Type preparer's name	Preparer's signature	Date	Check ☐ if self-employed	PTIN
Firm's name ▶			Firm's EIN ▶	
Firm's address ▶			Phone no.	

For Disclosure, Privacy Act, and Paperwork Reduction Act Notice, see instructions.   Cat. No. 11329W   Form **1040EZ** (2016)

Source: www.irs.gov

Even if your annual income does not meet the filing threshold, in my opinion, you should still file a tax return if you had federal income taxes withheld from your pay as you may be entitled to a refund. Employers are responsible for providing a W-2 form (shown below) to both employees and the IRS within a designated timeframe following the calendar year in which income was paid. This form is required by the IRS from employers to report wage and salary information on employees, and includes the amount of federal, state, and other taxes withheld from your paycheck.

Source: www.irs.gov

What the FICA?

Ha. FICA is the acronym for the Federal Insurance Contributions Act. This law paved the way for old age, survivors, and disability insurance (OASDI) taxes, also known as social security taxes; and hospital insurance taxes, better known as Medicare taxes. These taxes are meant to provide insurance benefits for the elderly, those with mental problems, and people with disabilities.

Why Do I Have to Pay for Social Security?

By law, most employees are required to pay social security tax. As indicated above, this is due to the FICA legislation. The current social security tax rate is 12.4%, of which one half (6.2%) is paid by your employer on your behalf and the other half (also 6.2%) is paid by you and withheld from your pay by your employer and sent to the IRS. Your portion of the 6.2% is limited to the first $127,200 [1] of income paid to you. If you have multiple jobs, this limit applies to each job.

If your employer treats you as an independent contractor, you are responsible for paying the full portion of social security tax.

1-This limit is applicable for 2017 and changes each year according to changes in the national average wage index.

Medicare

The Medicare tax rate, like the social security tax, is also paid by you and your employer. The current tax rate is 2.9%, which equates to 1.45% each. Unlike the limit placed on the amount of income subject to the social security tax, there is no limit on the amount of income subject to the Medicare tax rate.

That'll Never Happen to Me

You never know what might happen, and as a result, insurance is a way to be proactive on issues like health and wellness and to lessen the burden for when something does arise. Insurance is a big topic and is an ever-growing industry heavily regulated by the federal government.

Examples and descriptions for several insurance deductions are listed below:

1. *Medical, dental, and vision health premiums* – Health insurance coverage mostly available through your employer, if you choose to participate, that may be partially or fully paid for by the employer on your behalf.
2. *Life insurance* – Some companies offer life insurance coverage. A life insurance policy is a contract with an insurance company to provide a lump-sum payment to an individual designated by you (beneficiary) in exchange for premium payments.

Premiums are typically paid by the employer and/or at a small cost to the employee. The benefit amount (the amount payable upon death) may be less than, equal to, or greater than your salary. Employer-sponsored life insurance is often categorized as one size fits all with all employees receiving the same type of coverage with typically no medical exams. Group insurance provided in this manner is typically considered term life insurance, which is insurance that provides a stated benefit upon death of the policy owner.

3. *Supplemental life insurance* – An additional life insurance benefit option is sometimes offered by employers. The one size fits all insurance policy may not be enough to meet your coverage needs in the event that you become deceased. As such, you may need to obtain additional coverage. This additional coverage may be an option from your employer; however, you are not limited to obtaining it from your employer as you can also obtain this coverage from an outside insurance agency.

4. *Accidental Death & Dismemberment (AD&D) Insurance* – This is insurance coverage offered to employees to cover accidental death and dismemberment, including the loss of use of body parts or functions (limbs, speech, hearing, or eyesight), and is paid to the beneficiary if the cause of death is deemed an accident.

5. *Short- and long-term disability insurance* – Employers may offer short-term and long-term disability insurance, or one of these options. This insurance coverage is designed to replace income due to a serious illness or injury that prevents you from working for a period of time (typically three to six months). Long term coverage is similarly provided to replace income for the same reasons for an extended period of time and occurs for six months or greater. Each is paid for a short period of time after you run out of sick leave and may be less than or equal to your income.

A Penny a Day Keeps Your Future Safe

Many companies offer ways in which employees can save up for their future. Options like a 401(k) or pension plans are the most popular. According to the IRS, a 401(k) is basically a feature of a qualified profit-sharing plan (also known as a defined contribution plan) that allows employees to contribute a portion of their wages to individual accounts. These contributions are usually treated as deferred wages (elective deferrals) and are not subject to federal income tax withholding at the time of deferral and are not reported as taxable income on the individual income tax return of the employee. A pension plan is a defined benefit plan which guarantees a set amount of monthly income in retirement based on your pay (salary) and years of service. For many, the longer you work, the more your retirement benefits will be. Social Security is considered a defined benefit plan.

Both retirement saving options are typically deducted from an employee's income on a pre-tax (before tax) basis and may be matched by the employer up to a specified percentage of income. One important item worth mentioning is that if you are planning on working with a company for only a limited time, pay attention to the years required to be fully vested.

"What does it mean to be fully vested?" Well, let's say you were hired by a company and you contribute three percent (3%) to your 401(k). You've been with the company four (4) years now and you decide that it's time to move on to pursuing other options. You know that your employer matches your 401(k) contribution up to six percent (6%) and requires five (5) years of employment to be fully vested. Therefore, if you leave, your 401(k)-payout percentage would include the full percentage amount you contributed (3%) plus the prorated percentage contributed by your employer (3% x 4/5). The equation would look something like this:

Payout Percentage = 3% Employee Contribution + [3% Employer Contribution x (4 ÷ 5)]

$$= .03 + (.03 \times .8)$$
$$= .03 + (.024)$$
$$= .054$$
$$= 5.4\%$$

This means that your payout percentage for the amount con-tributed to the 401(k) by you and your employer would be 5.4%. It is important to build a contingency fund and with every pay-check, you should put a portion aside into a savings structure. You should also consider putting a portion or all of any pay increase you may receive into savings before you get use to spending it. There it blows! It seems no matter how much someone's paycheck increases, the more that person's expenses and cost of living increases. This is not necessarily the case with savvy savers or those who have been taught and practice these methods already.

Don't get surprised like Raine. That salary will sound wonderful when you receive your offer letter, but if you don't understand deductions and taxes you won't understand why your take home pay will be much less. Understanding your paycheck will help you know what salary to look for and help you save for your future.

Conclusion

Now that you have finished reading chapters 1 through 5, you should be ready to handle many of the challenges you may be faced with. To review, we have discussed the following:

1. Interviewing like a Boss
   - Having an effective resume, one tailored to the position you are applying for, will help you land an interview for the job you are applying.
   - A cover letter will help enhance your resume and allow you to point out why you are the best candidate for the job.
   - Showing up early and preparing will help you ace your interview.
   - Practice, Practice, Practice!

2. Workplace Habits
   - Show up on time and work your full shift.

- Learn to manage your workload. Doing this will help you avoid unnecessary stress and reduce your likelihood of working extra hours.
- Behave appropriately in the workplace and know your company's policies.
- Network with others. This can create opportunities for you.
- Dress appropriately.

3. Developing Yourself like a Boss
   - Identify your career goals.
   - Find a Mentor.
   - Develop a SWOT analysis that will help you identify your personal strengths and weaknesses, and develop a strategic plan for achieving your career goals.
   - Create an effective workplace brand.
   - Continue to develop your technical and personal skills.
   - Have a plan for handling tasks you don't know how to do.

4. What are you saying about Yourself?
   - Be careful what you post to your social media accounts.

- Make sure you have effective social skills. Don't get labeled as the person who is always speaking negatively about everything or the person who talks too much.

- Keep a positive attitude.

5. Where's my money?
   - Know how to identify how you are getting paid, hourly vs salary.
   - Understand your paycheck and all the deductions you see in your pay stub.
   - Save for your future!

For additional practice and examples, check out Beyond the Job Description: The Workbook. You can order your copy online at www.ChristinaAlva.com. We hope you have enjoyed this book and wish you lots of success in the workplace.

About the Authors

Christina Alva is a lead data analytics developer and supervisor for a large think tank company in the Washington, D.C. area. As a supervisor, she assists in hiring and developing new recruits. She is the CEO of Amazing Books, LLC, and a board member of the non-profit organization Coders Who Travel whose goal is to give back to the community by providing technical assistance and training to help others succeed in the programming industry. Aside from work, Christina loves writing, dancing, playing video games, and hanging out with friends and family.

Christina co-authored Beyond the Job Description with her best friend and sister, Camille Marbury, because she is passionate about helping new professionals succeed in the workplace. Follow Christina on Instagram @ChristinaNAlva or visit her website at www.ChristinaAlva.com to get more tips on how to succeed in the workplace.

Camille Marbury is a senior auditor for one of the world's largest publicly traded communications companies headquartered in Texas. In her position, she is responsible for conducting financial, operational, compliance, and regulatory audits to assure effective and efficient operations within the company for management and stakeholders. Camille is a certified life coach and has held numerous volunteer positions, including the roles of chair and president, for various nonprofit organizations.

In her spare time, Camille enjoys mentoring, dancing, writing, singing, watching movies, traveling, meeting new people, spending time with family and friends, and encouraging others. Camille continues to enjoy journeying through life, especially with her lifetime friend and sister, Christina Alva, co-author of Beyond the Job Description. Camille's decision to co-author Beyond the Job Description was based on her endless pursuit of passing on knowledge to others. You can follow Camille on Instagram @CamilleMarbury.